RISING
SEAS

FLOODING, CLIMATE CHANGE
AND OUR NEW WORLD

Text by Keltie Thomas

Art By Belle Wuthrich **and** Kath Boake W.

A FIREFLY BOOK

Published by Firefly Books Ltd. 2018
Copyright © 2018 Firefly Books Ltd.
Text copyright © 2018 Keltie Thomas

First printing

Library of Congress Control Number: 2017954639

Library and Archives Canada Cataloguing in Publication
Thomas, Keltie, author
Rising seas : flooding, climate change and our new
world / text by Keltie Thomas ; art by Belle Wuthrich and
Kath Boake W.
Includes bibliographical references and index.
ISBN 978-0-228-10021-8 (softcover).--ISBN 978-0-228-10022-5
(hardcover)
1. Sea level--Juvenile literature. 2. Floods--Juvenile literature.
3. Climatic changes--Juvenile literature. I. Boake, Kathy, illustrator
II. Wuthrich, Belle, 1989-, illustrator III. Title.
GC89.T46 2018   j551.45'8   C2017-906177-1

Published in the United States by
Firefly Books (U.S.) Inc.
P.O. Box 1338, Ellicott Station
Buffalo, New York 14205

Published in Canada by
Firefly Books Ltd.
50 Staples Avenue, Unit 1
Richmond Hill, Ontario L4B 0A7

Cover and interior design: Belle Wuthrich

Printed in China

Canada We acknowledge the financial support of the Government of Canada.

Contents

EARTH IS GOING ⌐ UNDER ⌐

SURE, WE CALL OUR PLANET "EARTH." But a more fitting name for our one and only home in the universe would be Water. More than two-thirds of our planet lies under water, and all life on Earth depends on the thirst-quenching stuff to survive. What's more, water shapes Earth like nothing else.

Climate is the expected weather over a long time, such as a cold, snowy winter. *Weather*, on the other hand, is the temperature, rain, wind, and other atmospheric conditions that pop up from minute to minute or day to day.

WATER—THE EARTH SHAPER

AS RIVERS AND STREAMS flow down from mountains, water carves out grooves and valleys. In times when temperatures dip, such as the last Ice Age, some of that water freezes into huge sheets of ice called glaciers.

As glaciers grow, they flow over land. They pick up rocks and dirt and drag them along for the ride, gouging as they go. Later, when temperatures climb, the glaciers melt, dumping the rocks and dirt in piles or sheets. And the meltwater fills the gouges and holes, forming lakes and ponds.

Then there's the ocean. The mighty ocean rolls on and off shore, shaping coastlines as it comes and goes. In times when temperatures rise, changing our planet's climate, the sea also rises. The seawater flows farther inland, changing the face of the Earth.

This is one of those times. Since 1880, the global average sea level has risen 8 inches (20.32 cm). And it's still climbing. In about 80 years—or by the time your grandchildren are adults—scientists think the sea might be as much as 8.2 feet (2.5 m) or more higher than today.

WHAT'S THE BIG DEAL?

AS THE SEA CREEPS inland, water floods and submerges coastal lands. Today, many coastal areas are jam-packed with people. About a hundred million people live within 3 feet (0.9 m) of average high tide. And another hundred million live within the watery reach of storm surges.

New Orleans
Population: 391,495

Nuuk, Greenland
Population: 17,600

Miami Beach
Population: 91,917

Lower Manhattan, NY
Population: 49,000

LIVING ON THE EDGE

ALL OF THESE PEOPLE living in coastal areas means the rising water will push millions out of house and home. Along the way, it'll also claim cropland and seep into rivers and groundwater, destroying resources that feed and quench the thirst of the world. Where in the world will all those homeless go? Where in the world will food and drinking water come from to replace those lost resources? And just how did we get into this mess?

COUNTRIES IN THE DANGER ZONE

WHERE ARE MILLIONS OF PEOPLE in the most danger from rising sea levels? Check out the countries with the highest populations living below predicted sea level rise (SLR) for global warming of 3.6°F to 7.2°F (2–4°C).

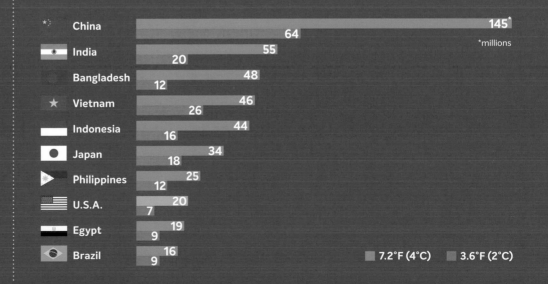

Country	7.2°F (4°C)	3.6°F (2°C)
China	145*	64
India	55	20
Bangladesh	48	12
Vietnam	46	26
Indonesia	44	16
Japan	34	18
Philippines	25	12
U.S.A.	20	7
Egypt	19	9
Brazil	16	9

*millions

■ 7.2°F (4°C)   ■ 3.6°F (2°C)

WHAT'S DRIVING SEA RISE?

I'm under the weather, er, sea. I've got a fever of 103!

WHAT'S UP, DOC?

HUMANS, THAT'S WHAT! As we burn oil, gas, and coal for energy to run our cars and factories, heat our homes, and light the world, carbon dioxide (CO_2) is emitted.

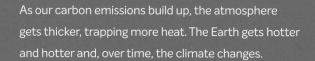

As our carbon emissions build up, the atmosphere gets thicker, trapping more heat. The Earth gets hotter and hotter and, over time, the climate changes.

Our carbon emissions build up in the atmosphere—a thin layer of gases around Earth that traps heat from the Sun.

And humans are multiplying. Today, 7.3 billion of us live on Earth. By 2050, we're expected to number 9.7 billion and, by 2100, 11.2 billion. Just imagine the impact that will have on carbon emissions!

HOW DO RISING TEMPERATURES = RISING OCEANS?

1 **AS WATER WARMS, IT EXPANDS, RISING UP.** For each 1.8°F (1°C) that world temperatures climb, water expansion makes the sea climb nearly 1.3 feet (0.4 m). Say your mom is average height. That's nearly enough to reach her kneecaps.

2 **GLACIERS CAN MELT, ADDING WATER TO THE OCEAN.** If all the glaciers in the world melted, scientists think the sea would rise about 2 feet (0.6 m). That's about the height of a German shepherd.

3 **ICE SHEETS LIKE THOSE IN GREENLAND AND ANTARCTICA CAN MELT, ADDING WATER TO THE OCEAN.**

If the ice sheet in Greenland had a complete meltdown, scientists think the sea would rise 20 feet (6 m). That's about three times the height of an average NBA player.

If the ice sheet in Antarctica melted, scientists think the sea would rise 180 to 197 feet (55–60 m). That's almost a whole head and shoulders taller than the Statue of Liberty.

HOW FAST WILL THE SEA RISE?

THAT'S THE CRUCIAL QUESTION. In fact, some scientists call it "the trillion dollar question." Since 1880, sea level has risen about 8 inches (15 cm). In the last 20 years, the rate of sea rise has almost doubled, and scientists expect it to keep going up. Will it rise:

SLOW 'N STEADY? A rise of 1 or 2 feet (0.3–0.6 m) every 100 years might give coastal cities and towns time to adapt.

OR ... FAST 'N ACCELERATED

A rise of 10 feet (3 m) every 10 years would force those living in coastal towns and cities to pick up stakes and move. Not only would millions of people lose their homes, but the cost to governments could also be trillions of dollars.

AND THE ANSWER IS ... No one knows. It depends on how soon and how fast the ice sheets in Greenland and Antarctica melt. And that's a wet 'n wild puzzle that scientists around the world are trying to solve (see pages 48–49 for more about this).

WHAT IF WE STOP EMITTING CO$_2$ TODAY?

THE EARTH'S AVERAGE TEMPERATURE and oceans will still continue to rise. Carbon hangs around for hundreds, even thousands of years, and as it hangs out, its effects grow.

That means that whatever amount of carbon has built up today will continue to warm the Earth over time. Say, for example, we see a two-degree jump in temperature from the built-up carbon today. As it hangs out in the atmosphere, that carbon may eventually raise the temperature another two degrees, even though no more carbon is being emitted.

WHAT NOW, EARTHLINGS?

NEVER BEFORE have the actions of humans been able to change the sea level on Earth. According to scientists, we've entered the "Anthropocene", a new era in Earth's history in which human activities are a major force that affects the environment and climate of the planet.

LOSERS 'R US

LIKE IT OR NOT, no one has more to lose from the rising water than we do. The Earth's coastal areas, which are in the direct "line of flood," are home to hundreds of millions of people. About 136 coastal cities have populations of more than one million people, and at least 15 of these cities have populations of more than 10 million.

If sea level were to rise 19.6 feet (6 m), the areas shaded in light blue would be underwater.

NATIONS ON THE BRINK

THERE ARE ALSO LOW-LYING island nations that the rising sea could wipe right off the face of the Earth. If these countries disappear completely, where will their citizens find refuge? What countries will give them shelter, passports, and other citizenship rights? Where will their people find the food and drink they need? These are all questions that countries and groups around the world are working on, but there are no easy answers.

FUTURE IN OUR HANDS

JUST AS OUR ACTIONS influence sea level rise and climate change on Earth, they can also influence how high the water and temperatures go. This means that what we do now—either to add to or cut down our carbon emissions—can shape the planet's future. And we've begun to take steps to do just that. In 2015, countries around the world agreed to reduce carbon emissions to keep global warming "well below" 3.6°F (2°C). Coastal cities and communities are also putting together local game plans to tackle sea level rise head-on.

WHAT'S YOUR SLR GAME PLAN?

IN THE FACE OF SEA LEVEL RISE, coastal communities can use the following strategies to prepare for a watery future:

PROTECT by building walls, levees, and other structures to stop rising water from getting in.

ADAPT by raising buildings, roads, and other structures so they stay above the rising water.

RELOCATE by pulling up stakes and moving to higher ground, out of reach of the rising water.

FAST FORWARD TO 2100

HOW WILL TODAY'S RISING TEMPERATURES and sea levels change the face of the Earth in your lifetime and beyond? What countries, cities, and communities are in the "line of the flood," and what game plans do they have in development to meet it? Check out the watery hotspots on the map below. And to glimpse the future that scientists predict for them, just turn the page and dive into this book.

MAP KEY:

● Low-lying island
■ Low-lying coast
∼ Delta (where rivers flow into the sea)
▢ Ice sheet

MIAMI BEACH

GROUND ZERO

WELCOME TO "GROUND ZERO" of the rising sea. That's what people call South Florida, and no city there is at greater risk than Miami Beach. Not only is seawater inching onto shore, but it's also spurting up from the ground. This photo illustration shows what the city's future may look like as the sea rises.

SPOTLIGHT ON ...

MIAMI BEACH

FLORIDA

Biscayne Bay

MIAMI BEACH

Atlantic Ocean

Off the coast of South Florida, the city of Miami Beach lies on a barrier island just 1 mile (1.6 km) wide. The Atlantic Ocean roars in on one shore while Biscayne Bay laps the other.

WHERE IN THE WORLD?
South Florida

HOME TO: 91,917 people

SIZE: 7.63 square miles (20 sq km)

SEA-FEARING HEIGHTS: most of the city is barely 2 feet (0.6 m) above the sea

BY 2100, SEA LEVEL RISE MAY AFFECT: nearly 2 million people in Miami–Dade County

SLR GAME PLAN? P for protect and **A** for adapt

ONLY IN MIAMI BEACH: a mayor who "floated" into office with a TV ad of himself paddling through the city's rain-flooded streets in a kayak

⚓ HERE AND NOW

WHERE CAN YOU SEE FISH SWIMMING IN THE STREETS? In the city
of Miami Beach after a flood. A recent study shows that sea level rise has
tripled in South Florida since 2006, and the number of floods has shot up.
In fact, the sea is rising 10 times faster here than the global average. The
South Florida area is made of limestone rock that is full of holes, like Swiss
cheese. So when the rising sea floods in, water and fish travel through the
ground and bubble up to the surface. That means that building levees, or
seawalls, like those in the Netherlands (pages 26–27), won't keep the sea
at bay here. The water will just gush through the ground under the wall
and surge up on the other side.

⏩ FAST FORWARD TO THE FUTURE

IF OUR CARBON EMISSIONS continue unchecked, the rising sea will bury Miami Beach and much of South Florida underwater in 80 years or less. And even if we make huge cuts to these emissions, large chunks of the area will still be flooded. But concerned citizens are doing their best to come up with a solution. In Miami Beach, the local government is rebuilding streets at higher levels to keep them dry at high tide. They're raising the height of seawalls, shoring up sand dunes, and creating green spaces to absorb water and carbon dioxide like sponges. And they're also putting in gigantic underground pumps to suck up water from the street and dump it into Biscayne Bay. But the pumps can't keep up with extreme flooding like that from Hurricane Irma (see below).

City at work: Miami Beach is raising this street to help keep the roadway above water.

> Millions of years ago, Earth was much hotter than today. The average global sea level was much higher, and the land that is now Florida was completely underwater.

Hurricane Irma's Whirl of Destruction

As Hurricane Irma brewed over the Atlantic Ocean in 2017, it grew to be more than 400 miles (644 km) wide with winds up to 185 miles per hour (298 kmh), making it the strongest Atlantic storm on record. Irma whirled through the Caribbean, flattening homes, hurling cars, and killing several people. Government officials in Florida ordered people in the Keys, Miami Beach, and other coastal areas to evacuate. Irma hit Florida with heavy rain, roaring wind, and storm surges, tearing apart homes in the Keys, flooding Miami Beach and other coastal cities, and knocking out power for more than 6.8 million people. As global temperatures rise, scientists say to expect more extreme storms like this.

SOMETHING'S EATING ...

NEW ORLEANS

SOMETHING'S GOBBLING UP the city, and it's not a hurricane like Katrina, which demolished New Orleans in 2005. Nope. It's the rising sea. Every hour, the water devours a nearby land chunk the size of a football field. According to scientists, there's no way to stop it from eventually polishing off the whole southeast coast of Louisiana.

SPOTLIGHT ON ...
NEW ORLEANS

WHERE IN THE WORLD? The coast of Louisiana on the Gulf of Mexico

HOME TO: 391,495 people

SIZE: 169.42 square miles (439 sq km)

SEA-FEARING HEIGHTS: lowest point is 8 feet (2.4 m) below sea level

BY 2100, SEA LEVEL RISE MAY THREATEN: the city's entire population

SLR GAME PLAN? P for protect, **A** for adapt, and **R** for relocate

PRICELESS TREASURE: Bayou Savage National Wildlife Refuge, the largest urban wildlife refuge in the United States, where American alligators, white-tailed deer, and other animals hang out, and some 30,000 waterfowl flock in and out

NEW ORLEANS

FLORIDA

Gulf of Mexico

New Orleans lies on the coast of Louisiana. Can you see the "boot" that sticks out into the Gulf of Mexico?

14

⚓ HERE AND NOW

LOOK OUT, BELOW! New Orleans is sinking—and how. The city is falling faster than any major coastal area on Earth. Some chunks are dropping an inch every two and half years. At this rate, it'll sink nearly 3 feet (1 m) by 2100. As if that's not enough to whet the rising sea's appetite, about half the city barely bobs above current sea level. The other half lies below it. When researchers plug these figures into apps that map what the area will look like in 2100, New Orleans and Louisiana's "boot" are under-water. In fact, the sea has already swallowed so much land, people say the coast no longer looks like a boot.

▶▶ FAST FORWARD TO THE FUTURE

NEW ORLEANS WON'T GO DOWN without a fight. Louisiana has a plan to protect the threatened coast-line. The plan calls for rebuilding levees and pump stations as well as restoring islands to act as natural seawalls and wetlands to act as water "speed bumps." The plan also includes raising and flood-proofing buildings, and having people move to higher ground. Still, as scientists learn more about sea level rise and how to predict it, the plan needs regular revamping to avoid missing the "high-water mark." Otherwise, the sea will top the levees and flood on in.

In 2005, Hurricane Katrina flooded 80 percent of New Orleans. Will boating in the streets become the new normal as the rising sea flows in?

🐟 The Big Stink, er, Sink 🐟

Why, oh why, is New Orleans sinking? The city lies at the mouth of the mighty Mississippi River. Long ago, the river flowed into the area, carrying sand, silt, and clay. And so the river built up the land. Plants and trees in nearby marshes also helped out as they shed their leaves to make soil. After a disastrous flood in 1927, levees were built to protect the area north of the city. The levees stopped the flow of sand, silt, and clay. And a drainage system began pumping water out of the soil. This created pockets of air in the soil. The dead plant parts then decayed and the soil sank. Without new sand, silt, and clay flowing in, the land kept sinking. And as canals were built, the land sank further. Even if the river were to start carrying sand, silt, and clay again, it couldn't bring enough for the city to withstand the rising sea.

NEW YORK

PAINTING THE CITY BLUE?

IF NEW YORK HARBOR rises all around her, as shown in this photo illustration, will the Statue of Liberty keep her toes dry? As the rising sea charges in near the New York Stock Exchange, will the Wall Street Bull keep its head above water? Will these statues continue to stand for the hopes and dreams of many New Yorkers, or will they become symbols of the city's sinking fortunes?

SPOTLIGHT ON ...

NEW YORK

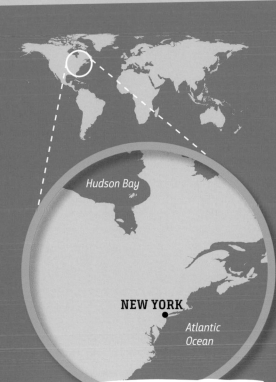

Hudson Bay

Atlantic Ocean

NEW YORK

WHERE IN THE WORLD?
East coast of the United States

HOME TO:
8,550,405 people

SIZE: 302.64 square miles (784 sq km)

SEA-FEARING HEIGHTS: some parts are only 5 feet (1.5 m) above sea level; others are at sea level

BY 2100, SEA LEVEL RISE MAY THREATEN: 400,000 people

SLR GAME PLAN? P for protect and **A** for adapt

PRICELESS TREASURE: Statue of Liberty, a gift from France that has become a worldwide symbol of freedom

As sea levels rise, the Big Apple could take a big bath. New York City has the longest coastline of any city in the United States.

Not much stands between Manhattan, the most densely populated area of New York City, and rising water.

⚓ HERE AND NOW

SEEING AS LADY LIBERTY'S TOES are perched 154 feet (47 m) above the harbor, the rising water's unlikely to reach them—even by 2100. Not so for the Wall Street Bull (see page 17). Standing near the shore of lower Manhattan, the bull is set to meet the rising sea head on. If only it could beat the water back. In New York City (NYC), seawater is climbing twice as high as the global average. What's up with the water there? Scientists think there are two things going on. One, changes in ocean currents, which carry tons of water around the sea, are piling up water on the coast of NYC. Two, the city is sinking. During the last ice age, glaciers pressed down heavily on nearby land. In response, the surrounding land, including present-day NYC, bulged. Once the glaciers melted, the bulge began to sink. And it hasn't hit bottom yet.

⏩ FAST FORWARD TO THE FUTURE

THREE FEET, SIX FEET ... however much global sea level jumps by 2100 and beyond, the water's bound to jump higher in NYC (see page 16). So the city is taking steps to prepare. Back in 2008, then mayor Michael Bloomberg put a group of scientists together with city planners. The scientists' job was to predict local SLR, and the city planners set about looking for ways to protect local buildings and adapt to the challenges—for example, building seawalls, adjusting building code or rules, raising key buildings, and restoring wetlands to buffer rising water. Nevertheless, if our carbon emissions continue at their current rate, huge coastal areas of NYC will end up underwater, including all but the tip of the tail of the Wall Street Bull (see photo illustration, right).

Will the Wall St. Bull need scuba gear when the rising sea rolls in?

The super-strong winds of Hurricane Sandy raised havoc and the sea, wrecking whole neighborhoods in Manhattan.

When Hurricane Sandy Hit NYC in 2012 ...

All sea broke loose. A 13-foot-high (4 m) gush of seawater stormed over the seawalls of Manhattan, spilling onto highways and city streets. The seawater flooded roadways, tunnels, subway stations, and Wall Street's power system. In fact, the flooding knocked out power for part of Manhattan. New Yorkers got a glimpse of how sea level rise could affect the city and stepped up their plans to tackle SLR. As then mayor Michael Bloomberg declared, "We cannot, and will not, abandon our waterfront."

NOVA SCOTIA

BEACON TO THE FUTURE

WHEN THE RISING SEA comes crashing in, waves will roll. And the lighthouse at Peggy's Cove, shown in this photo illustration, will be on the frontline. Not only is it perched on the edge of the ocean, but it also keeps watch over surging surf.

SPOTLIGHT ON ...

NOVA SCOTIA

NEW
BRUNSWICK

PRINCE
EDWARD ISLAND

MAINE

NOVA SCOTIA

Bay of
Fundy

Atlantic Ocean

No matter where you are in Nova Scotia,
you're never far from the sea. The province
is virtually surrounded by the Atlantic Ocean.

WHERE IN THE WORLD?
East coast of Canada,
next to the Atlantic
Ocean

HOME TO:
943,002 people

SIZE:
20,593.92 square miles
(53,338 sq km)

SEA-FEARING HEIGHTS:
0 feet (0 m) at the
Atlantic Ocean

**BY 2100, SEA LEVEL RISE
MAY THREATEN:** more
than 660,100 people

SLR GAME PLAN?
P for protect, **A** for
adapt, **R** for relocate

PRICELESS TREASURE:
Bay of Fundy, where
the highest tides in the
world once reached a
record-setting height
of 71 feet (21.6 m)
due to high winds,
abnormally low air
pressure, and a
spring tide

⚓ HERE AND NOW

NOVA SCOTIA FACES extreme exposure. The east coast of the province fronts the open ocean, meeting the rising water head on. Unlike coastal areas of bays and gulfs, there's no natural shelter from the water there. The sea slams onto the shore and barrels right in. In fact, seawater is rising twice as fast in Nova Scotia as the global average. Since 1920, the water has crept up about 1 foot (30 cm). If you'd been standing on the shore all that time, the water would have risen between your toes, over your feet, above your ankles, and nearly to your knees or higher. By 2100, scientists think seawater will climb another 2.5 to 4.5 feet (70–140 cm). Say you were to stay put on shore till then. The water would creep up your legs, past your hips, and to your belly button. It might even climb up above your head and then some!

1998 high-tide level

1973 high-tide level

Want to see some cold, hard evidence of the rising sea? Look no further. On a stone wall at the Fortress of Louisburg in Nova Scotia, there's a ring that ships tied up to in the 1740s. That ring is nearly one and half feet (50 cm) below today's high-tide mark.

▶▶ FAST FORWARD TO THE FUTURE

WHAT CAN YOU DO when the rising sea's beating down your shore? Nova Scotians know they can't ignore the writing on that fortress wall. Not only is the ocean rising, but the land they're living on is sinking, which increases sea level rise. What's more, Nova Scotia is prone to tropical storms that cause floods. As the sea rises, the storm surges that cause these floods will soar higher, reaching farther and farther inland. That's a dangerous problem in a province where most cities and towns are on the coast. So Nova Scotia is planning for the future by cutting down carbon emissions, topping up seawalls, and passing laws that require new buildings to be set back from the shore and built well above the high-water mark.

Ocean Jumps Up

"No sudden moves." Try telling that to the ocean and you're likely to get a splash in the face. In 2009, the ocean made a sudden jump along the east coast of North America. The water rose more than 4 inches (10 cm) from New York to Newfoundland; in Halifax, Nova Scotia, it soared 4.3 inches (11 cm). And it didn't drop down for more than a year. What was up with that? Researchers found that the Gulf Stream, which carries water along the east coast of North America, was weaker than usual. Thus, the water was able to rise higher as the Gulf Stream passed through. As the Earth heats up, scientists think this will happen more often. So we can expect more sudden jumps in sea level rise to make a splash.

LENNOX ISLAND

SWEPT AWAY

IT'S NO SECRET THE RISING SEA IS taking Lennox Island under. Once, when an elder asked the Mi'kmaq community where they saw the island in 25 to 50 years, a little kid piped up with "a bridge going nowhere." The kid meant that the Lennox Island Bridge would have nowhere to go.

⚓ HERE AND NOW

SIGNS OF THE RISING SEA are everywhere in Prince Edward Island (P.E.I.). And no one sees them more plainly than the Lennox Island First Nation, who have lived here, off the coast of the mainland, for thousands of years. Fish swim where people used to play baseball. Every year, large chunks of the red sandy shore disappear. And as the sea swallows the chunks whole, it spits up ancient artifacts, such as spears, arrowheads, and stone tools made by the Mi'kmaq nation's ancestors. Since 1816, the sea has polished off about 300 football fields worth of land, inching ever closer to houses that used to be set back from the shore—so close that some homeowners joke that they'll soon be scuba diving instead of driving, or wearing a lifejacket to bed. But that doesn't mean they're treating sea level rise as a laughing matter. And they aren't waiting around for the world to cut the engine of sea level rise by lowering carbon emissions either.

Residents use rock to reinforce the shore line in parts of Lennox Island. Rising sea levels and coastal erosion threaten the Mi'Kmaq community, which has seen a major loss of landmass in the last 50 years.

▶▶ FAST FORWARD TO THE FUTURE

THE LENNOX ISLAND First Nation is fast at work to make sure the rising water doesn't wash away their past and future. Made of sand and sandstone, the low-lying island erodes easily in water. Knowing this, the Mi'kmaq First Nation has ordered a number of scientific studies to explore when and where the rising sea will take over the island. Some studies predict that half of Lennox Island may be underwater by 2065. And the nation is using these scientific findings to plan for the future. For example, they're shoring up sacred burial grounds to protect them from the current threat of the water. They've also bought land on mainland P.E.I. to move to when the rising water makes it impossible to live on Lennox Island.

Playing with CLIVE

"My house is gone!" gasp people as they play with CLIVE—Coastal Impacts Visualization Environment. Born in a lab and developed with help from the Mi'kmaq Confederacy of P.E.I, the video game gives users a glimpse into the future. Using a video game controller, they fly over a 3-D map of P.E.I., exploring the impact of rising water 30, 60, or 90 years from now. For example, CLIVE reveals that the sea threatens to damage the sewage lagoon on Lennox Island. This glimpse then allows the Lennox Island First Nation to plan to relocate or protect the site. Lab developers are also using flying drones to photograph First Nation communities in P.E.I. to create sea level rise simulations that can help them plan for the future.

SPOTLIGHT ON ...
LENNOX ISLAND

The Lennox Island Bridge to and from the mainland is the only way on and off the island by foot or by car.

WHERE IN THE WORLD?
Malpeque Bay off the coast of Prince Edward Island in Canada

HOME TO:
about 450 people

SIZE: 4.74 square miles (12 sq km)

SEA-FEARING HEIGHTS:
on average the island is just 13 feet (4 m) above sea level

BY 2100, SEA LEVEL RISE MAY THREATEN:
the island's entire population

SLR GAME PLAN?
P for protect and
R for relocate

PRICELESS TREASURE:
arrowheads and other artifacts made by Indigenous peoples who have lived on the island for 10,000 years

GREENLAND
ON THE MELT

GREEN IT'S NOT. There are no forests and almost no farmland on Greenland—and a huge ice sheet covers four-fifths of the island. Around 980 CE, Norwegian explorer Erik the Red gave Greenland its bogus name to lure settlers. Today, its ice draws many scientists exploring how glaciers and ice sheets melt.

SPOTLIGHT ON ...
GREENLAND

WHERE IN THE WORLD? Between the Arctic and Atlantic Oceans

HOME TO: 57,733 people

SIZE: 836,330.48 square miles (2,166,086 sq km)

SEA-FEARING HEIGHTS: lowest point is 0 feet (0 m) at the Atlantic Ocean

BY 2100, SEA LEVEL RISE MAY THREATEN: an unknown number of people

SLR GAME PLAN? A for adapt and **R** for relocate

ONLY IN GREENLAND: the glacier that sunk the *Titanic*. Scientists think the iceberg that smashed into the huge cruise ship in 1912 broke off Greenland's Jakobshavn glacier.

GREENLAND
Arctic Ocean
Atlantic Ocean
HAWAII
AUSTRALIA

Greenland lies halfway between Hawaii and Australia.

Every year, Greenland's ice sheet loses enough water to fill 110 million Olympic-size swimming pools.

⚓ HERE AND NOW

CAN YOU PICTURE a sheet of ice nearly as big as Mexico? Mind-boggling, isn't it? But that's the size of Greenland's ice sheet. And it's not thin like the sheets on your bed. In fact, in some places, it's 10,000 feet (3,048 m) deep. That's like eight Empire State Buildings stacked on top of each other. But as the average global temperature rises, the giant ice sheet is melting. Every summer, the edges and the top melt. The top meltwater seeps into deep cracks, flowing to the bottom of the glacier where it forms a film between the ice and bedrock. Some scientists wonder if this film might speed up the ice sheet's slide toward the sea. And the meltwater from the edges? That flows into the sea, adding to sea level rise.

▶▶ FAST FORWARD TO THE FUTURE

TRY PICTURING GREENLAND IN 2100 and things get fuzzy. The good news is that scientists don't think Greenland's ice sheet will melt away during your lifetime. That's a relief, because if the whole sheet melts, it'll raise sea level by nearly 20 feet (6 m). But what scientists don't know is how fast it will melt—and they've noticed that glaciers at the edges of the ice sheet are melting at record-breaking speeds. As these glaciers melt, they break up, dumping icebergs and water into the sea. They also move inland, exposing dark soil and bedrock. That means in the future, Greenland may have a smaller ice sheet surrounded by a dark ring of ice-free land. But just how far inland this dark ring will stretch is a mystery scientists are trying to solve.

Rubber Ducky, You're the One!

In 2008, a researcher dropped 90 rubber ducks into deep holes in Greenland's Jakobshavn glacier. Since rubber ducks stay afloat in the iciest of waters, they were the perfect agents to uncover the mystery of how glaciers melt into the sea. Or so the researcher thought. He labeled the ducks with his contact information so anyone who found one could tell him where it ended up. He also sent a football-sized probe to track the ducks' journey and send information about the guts of the glacier. But the probe didn't send data for long, likely because it got stuck in the ice. And the whereabouts of only two ducks came to light, when a fisher reported finding them in a nearby bay. The rest of the rubber duckies are still at large, and just how glaciers melt and slip into the sea remains a deep, dark mystery.

THE NETHERLANDS

SEABUSTERS LIKE NO OTHER

IF THE RISING SEA soaks your neighborhood, who ya gonna call? Seabusters! The people of the Netherlands—a.k.a. the Dutch—have been battling the sea for hundreds of years.

SPOTLIGHT ON ...
THE NETHERLANDS

WHERE IN THE WORLD? Western Europe, next to the North Sea

HOME TO: 16,947,904 people

SIZE: 13,086.16 square miles (33,893 sq km)

SEA-FEARING HEIGHTS: lowest point is Zuidplaspolder, nearly 23 feet (7 m) below sea level

BY 2100, SEA LEVEL RISE MAY THREATEN: 24,000 people, if safeguards are in place

SLR GAME PLAN? P for protect —or, as the Dutch say, "prevent"

ONLY IN THE NETHERLANDS: the Maeslant Barrier—floating gates as long as the Eiffel Tower that open and close to keep out the sea, which can pound with as much force as 350,000 strong men lugging 220 pounds (100 kg) each

The Netherlands faces the North Sea. Its capital city, Amsterdam, has 165 canals for streets.

⚓ HERE AND NOW

THE NETHERLANDS is named after its low-lying land. As early as 500 BCE, the Dutch built dikes—or long walls—along the coast to hold back the sea. Today, more than a quarter of the country lies below sea level. Without dikes, that area would be an underwater playground for fish. And that's not the only flood risk here. Three rivers meet in the Netherlands, which the Dutch have also lined with dikes. The result? The dikes are so effective at keeping out the sea that many residents have forgotten about the flood risk altogether. Is it any wonder that countries around the world are calling on the Dutch for their seabusting expertise?

▶▶ FAST FORWARD TO THE FUTURE

IMAGINE THAT THE NETHERLANDS had absolutely no protection from floods. By 2100, sea level rise would bury a huge chunk of it completely underwater. About half the country is less than 3 feet (1 m) above sea level. Even its present-day sea barriers wouldn't shut out the rising water completely. But this nation of seabusters is not about to let the sea gain any ground. The Netherlands has the world's most advanced plan to combat sea level rise. They're also looking to nature to beat the sea. For example, they're shoring up sand dunes to hold the sea back with a "Sand Engine"—a half-mile-long (0.8 km) strip of sand. By 2030 or so, they expect wind and sea currents to have spread this sand 6 miles (9.6 km) along the shore, creating a natural barrier. Go seabusters, go!

Kids Take on Mission Impossible

Your mission, should you choose to accept it, is to build a sand castle to withstand the incoming sea. Sound impossible? That's the challenge a competition in the Netherlands puts to kids ages 6 to 11. That way, the kids learn about building structures to resist floods firsthand. The kids dive in, building fishlike castles, castles with ditches, and castles like labyrinths. They also have expert dike builders, engineers, and water managers standing by to offer help. And once the tide rolls in, the battle begins. May the last castle standing win!

THE NILE DELTA

>POOF< GOES THE DELTA

THE LAND AT THE MOUTH of the Nile River may not be going up in smoke, but it's sure going down under water. And it's not the first time, either.

SPOTLIGHT ON ...
THE NILE DELTA

WHERE IN THE WORLD?
Coast of Egypt, along the Mediterranean Sea

HOME TO: two-thirds of Egypt's population—about 59 million

SIZE: 10,000 square miles (25,900 sq km)

SEA-FEARING HEIGHTS: large parts are less than 3.3 feet (1 m) above the sea, and some are below

BY 2100, SEA LEVEL RISE MAY THREATEN: at least 6,100,000 people

SLR GAME PLAN? P for protect and **R** for relocate

ONLY IN THE NILE DELTA: legend has it that Cleopatra's long-lost tomb is buried somewhere near the western edge

The Nile delta meets the Mediterranean Sea along the coast of Egypt.

Sunken City

Beyond the Nile delta, deep-sea divers have found sphinxes, statues, and the palace of Cleopatra, the queen of Egypt from 47 to 30 BCE. Just how these ancient ruins ended up under the sea is a wet and wild tale of how the Earth rumbles. In 331 BCE, the warrior king Alexander the Great founded the city of Alexandria on the coast of Egypt. Chances are no one knew the coast was slowly sinking into the sea. In 365 CE, an earthquake shook the city. And hot on its heels, a tidal wave ripped through, hurling water and ships over houses. Lots of quakes followed, jiggling the Earth's crust under ancient Alexandria. Over time, parts of the city slid into the ocean.

⚓ HERE AND NOW

THE NILE DELTA is vanishing right before our eyes. As the sea laps on shore, it's wiping the delta off the face of the Earth bit by bit. In some spots, the sea erodes as much as 328 feet (100 m) a year. Locals say some trees that sprouted on land now stand in water that's knee deep. As the sea creeps farther and farther into the Nile Valley, it devours precious farmland. Farmland that supports and feeds some 50 million people who call the area home. Farmland that's allowed people to live there for more than 5,000 years.

▶▶ FAST FORWARD TO THE FUTURE

HUGE HUNKS of the Nile delta will disappear under the rising sea. The delta is slowly sinking; large parts barely poke above sea level, and, apart from an offshore sand belt, nothing stands between the delta and the pounding water. With a rise of just 3 feet (1 m), scientists think the sea will bust up the sand belt, flood more than six million people out of their homes, and swamp 897,000 football fields worth of farmland. They also think the sea will seep into freshwater lagoons and groundwater, killing off freshwater fish and shrinking the supply of drinking water. In a country with more than 88 million mouths to feed, not to mention thirsts to quench, that means tough times lie ahead. For many people, the only way to survive may be to leave.

THE MALDIVES

HEADED FOR A WATERY GRAVE?

JUST HOW LOW CAN YOU GO? Nowhere lower than here. The Maldives is the flattest country on Earth. There's not one hill in the entire nation. That means there's nowhere to go when the sea rises.

Uz. Hassan Latheef
Minister of Human Resources, Youth and Sports

17 OCTOBER 2009
K. GIRIFUSHI
MALDIVES

Dr. Ibrahim Di...
Minister of Fisheries and A...

SPOTLIGHT ON ...
THE MALDIVES

WHERE IN THE WORLD?
Indian Ocean

HOME TO: 393,253 people

SIZE: 115.06 square miles (298 sq km)

SEA-FEARING HEIGHTS: lowest point is 0 feet (0 m) at the Indian Ocean

BY 2100, SEA LEVEL RISE MAY THREATEN: 179,000 people

SLR GAME PLAN? Relocate—move to higher ground

ONLY IN THE MALDIVES: a president and cabinet members who held an underwater meeting in scuba gear

ASIA

AFRICA

• THE MALDIVES

Indian Ocean

About 1,190 far-flung coral islands make up the Maldives in the Indian Ocean.

SOS to the World

How do you send an SOS to the world that your nation may be drowning? In 2009, the Maldivian government held a cabinet meeting under the sea (see page 30). The cabinet members asked the world to help all island nations by cutting back their carbon dioxide emissions.

Former Maldives president Mohamed Nasheed kicked off a cabinet meeting underwater to show the world what the future may hold for his country.

⚓ HERE AND NOW

WHITE SANDY BEACHES where palm trees sway and clear water laps on shore make the Maldives a hotspot for tourists. The island nation is also a hotspot for sea level rise, because 80 percent of the country is less than 3.3 feet (1 m) above the sea. Even now, yearly floods affect more than 90 of the nation's islands where people live.

▶▶ FAST FORWARD TO THE FUTURE

AS EARLY AS 2008, the Maldivian government was saving up to buy a new homeland. That way, the nearly 400,000 people who live there will have a place to go as the rising sea comes rolling in. Scientists predict that the whole country could be underwater before 2100. To protect their homeland, islanders are looking after groundwater, collecting rainwater, and mounting new buildings high above ground.

Endangered Islands

The Maldives aren't the only islands that the rising sea may put under. Check out the following list of "endangered islands" that are home and country to people around the world today.

Pacific Ocean	Atlantic Ocean	Indian Ocean	Persian Gulf
☒ Marshall Islands	☒ Bahamas	☒ Maldives	☒ Bahrain
☒ Kiribati	☒ Cape Verde	☒ Seychelles	
☒ Tuvalu	☒ Trinidad & Tobago		
☒ Nauru			

MUMBAI

CITY OF FLOODS

WHEN IT RAINS, IT FLOODS! During the monsoon season, a heavy downpour in Mumbai can submerge city streets in water waist deep. As average temperatures and sea levels climb around the world, life in this bustling city is becoming even soggier. Will rising water flood Mumbai Harbour and rush through the Gateway to India, as in this photo illustration?

SPOTLIGHT ON …

MUMBAI

WHERE IN THE WORLD? West coast of India next to the Arabian Sea

HOME TO: about 20 million people

SIZE: 232.82 square miles (603 sq km)

SEA-FEARING HEIGHTS: lowest point is just above sea level

BY 2100, SEA LEVEL RISE MAY THREATEN: about 11 million people if global temperatures rise 7.2°F (4°C) and carbon emissions aren't cut

SLR GAME PLAN? A for adapt

PRICELESS TREASURE: ancient rock art in the "City of Caves" on Elephanta Island

CHINA
PAKISTAN
NEPAL
INDIA
● MUMBAI
Arabian Sea
Bay of Bengal
SRI LANKA

Mumbai, India's largest city, lies low and juts out into the Arabian Sea, within easy reach of rising water.

Walking is faster than driving in parts of Mumbai. But monster traffic jams haven't put the brakes on the city's fast-growing population.

⚓ HERE AND NOW

MUMBAI MIGHT NOT BE THE WETTEST place on Earth, but it's close.* Heavy rains flood the city almost every year. July and August are the wettest months, when half the city's annual rainfall can swamp the streets in just two or three downpours. And there's nowhere for much of that rainwater to go. For starters, large parts of the city lie below the high-tide levels that occur during storms. This allows seawater to enter the city's drains, creeks, streams, and ponds and prevents rainwater from draining. Secondly, the city is built on seven islands. As the city grew, marshes and creeks between the islands, where rainwater used to run off, were filled in to create one big island. Today, Greater Mumbai is known as Island City. Bridges connect the city to the mainland while the rising sea "watermarks" the city, climbing higher on shore here than is typical around the globe.

*Mawsynram, a mountain village in India, holds that title. It receives more rain a year than anywhere else. However, in 2017, Mumbai was submerged during record flooding.

⏩ FAST FORWARD TO THE FUTURE

NOT ONLY does much of Greater Mumbai lie just above sea level, but it's also surrounded by the sea on three sides. Recently, a group of local actors asked residents to consider the impact the rising sea might have on a popular waterfront tourist site, the Gateway of India (see left). Imagining the 85-foot-tall (26 m) stone gateway submerged under rising waters prompted the actors to grab people's attention and spark discussion. But the scene's not so far-fetched. Research shows that sea level rise will permanently flood large parts of Mumbai. Extreme rainfall is also expected to increase, which will, in turn, increase floods, destroy homes, and threaten people's lives. In fact, salt from seawater may even affect the stability of high-rise buildings. So the city of Mumbai is looking for ways to adapt to a waterlogged future.

Elephanta Caves

Nobody knows who carved the rock-cut "City of Caves" on Elephanta Island off the coast of Mumbai. Nor who sculpted the giant statues in the caves, one of which shows the three faces of the Hindu God Shiva—the Creator, the Preserver, and the Destroyer. Archaeologists think they were carved around 500 to 600 CE. The caves are just one of about 130 World Heritage sites around the globe that face long-term risk from the rising sea. These sites are treasures of spectacular art, architecture, and nature. If they're flooded, we may no longer be able to visit or study them. What's more, the sea may destroy them, wiping them out of the future.

Walk past this three-headed rock sculpture in the Elephanta Caves and you might feel like an ant. It's 20 feet (6 m) tall!

GUANGZHOU
DOWN IN THE DELTA

NO CITY IN THE WORLD has more coin to lose or people at risk from the rising sea than Guangzhou. The Guangzhou Circle may look like a supersized ancient Chinese coin, but it's a modern office building. As the sea rises, as shown in this photo illustration, will it coin a new era of sunken treasure?

SPOTLIGHT ON ...

GUANGZHOU

WHERE IN THE WORLD? Southern coast of China

HOME TO: about 14 million people

SIZE: 2,870.44 square miles (7,434 sq km)

SEA-FEARING HEIGHTS: most of the Pearl River delta is less than 3.3 feet (1 m) above sea level, and 13 percent is below sea level

BY 2100, SEA LEVEL RISE MAY THREATEN: more than 10 million people

SLR GAME PLAN? **P** for protect and **A** for adapt

PRICELESS TREASURE: Baiyun Mountain— the "lung of the city."

Guangzhou sits in the Pearl River delta of southern China.

Covered in green plants, Baiyun Mountain can take in 2,800 tons of CO_2 and pump out 2,100 tons of oxygen in one day.

The Guangzhou Circle is a landmark building. The building's shape is intended to echo a circular piece of jade, a good luck talisman.

⚓ HERE AND NOW

GUANGZHOU lies in the Pearl River delta, where three rivers meet. Not only is 13 percent of the delta below sea level, but most of the rest is less than 3.3 feet (1 m) above the sea. So the risk of sea level rise is "in your face" here. Since a fierce storm washed out part of the beach down by Pleasant Banyan Bay in 2008, seawater has been munching up the white sand through erosion. It's bitten off some 33-foot (10 m) chunks inland and is continuing to chomp away. Smaller beaches have disappeared altogether, and some locals even say they can see the water rising. Maybe that's because the sea is rising more than twice as fast here as the global average.

▶▶ FAST FORWARD TO THE FUTURE

GUANGZHOU MAY BE the world's biggest loser. According to the World Bank, no other major coastal city has as much money to lose from sea level rise as Guangzhou. In the flood-prone area around the low-lying city, many factories make goods that are shipped all over the world. Though dikes protect the area from sea level rise now, they may not be enough to hold back higher water. In fact, they might even add risk to sea level rise by drawing more people and business to the protected area. And if the dikes are not maintained and built higher as the risk climbs, the areas they protect can become more vulnerable. Ocean disasters already cost the area more than $1 billion per year. As sea levels rise, flooding will affect millions of people in the area. By 2050, the World Bank predicts that Guangzhou will lose $17.5 billion a year due to the impact of the rising sea. But maybe all this talk of money and disaster has been a jolt to the country's system. China is taking steps to cut back its carbon emissions, develop greener power sources, and plan for the rising tide.

Guangzhou sprawls across the Pearl River, which flows to the South China Sea. This bridge connects city neighborhoods via a six-lane roadway.

Fortune's Ebb and Flow

If cities could talk, Guangzhou might say, "The sea has been very, very good to me." The sprawling city is one of the wealthiest areas of China. You know that plastic slide at the park? That toy firetruck your little sister drives around? And that winter jacket of yours? Chances are they were made in Guangzhou, or another part of China. Not only is Guangzhou home to many factories that make a variety of toys and goods, but its seaside location also allows it to easily ship those goods all over the world. However, this wave of good fortune may ebb away in the costly face and danger of sea level rise. And shipping goods long distances is a big source of carbon emissions that fuel the climb of rising waters.

BANGLADESH
A WINDOW IN TIME

IF YOU WANT TO SEE Earth's future under a rising sea, look at this photo illustration of a busy intersection in Dhaka, the capital city of Bangladesh. A huge sculpture of a Shapla, or waterlily, floats quietly as the climbing water cuts off the daily swarm of cars and buses that snarl up the surrounding road (see inset photo). And if you head further south into the Ganges delta, the world's most crowded river delta, you won't need a photo illustration to see into the watery future.

SPOTLIGHT ON ...

BANGLADESH

Sandwiched between India and Myanmar, Bangladesh borders the Bay of Bengal.

WHERE IN THE WORLD? South Asia along the Bay of Bengal

HOME TO: more than 156 million people

SIZE: 50,258.92 square miles (130,170 sq km)

SEA-FEARING HEIGHTS: nearly a quarter of the country is less than 7 feet (2.1 m) above the sea

BY 2100, SEA LEVEL RISE MAY THREATEN: more than 15 million people

SLR GAME PLAN? A for adapt

PRICELESS TREASURE: two-thirds of the Sundarbans—the world's largest mangrove forest, where the last of the Bengal tigers roam

Life on the watery edge forces people to move inland to Dhaka. But heavy rainfall, overflowing rivers, and storm surges flood life in the big city, too.

⚓ HERE AND NOW

EVERYWHERE YOU LOOK in the Ganges delta, you'll see signs of the sea eating away, or eroding, the shoreline. Not to mention buildings ripped apart by the sea. Or uprooted palm trees growing in rivers where they've been tossed by the sea. Or once-green fields dusted white with salt by the sea. Then there's the freshwater that the sea has turned salty, and the farmland that the sea has left barren. And that's not all. The ocean floods this low-lying area so often that the effects mimic those of sea level rise. In fact, one study shows that high tides in Bangladesh are rising 10 times faster than the global average.

▶▶ FAST FORWARD TO THE FUTURE

BANGLADESH IS IN THE FAST LANE of sea level rise. First off, most of the country sits on low-lying river deltas. As land settles, deltas sink naturally, which can add to sea level rise. Secondly, some of the steps Bangladesh has taken for flood protection, such as building seawalls and draining water, have made the delta sink more, increasing the threat. If carbon emissions continue full throttle, the country's climate scientists and government think the sea will cover nearly one-fifth of the country by 2050, sending about 18 million people on the hunt for new homes. But the country's so crowded that there's nowhere for them to move. And one study predicts that by 2100 the sea could rise four times higher here than the global average. No wonder Bangladesh is calling for countries around the world to make swift, deep cuts to carbon emissions. It's also building early warning systems and concrete shelters for floods, and looking for ways to grow crops in salty water to prepare for the day when the sea washes away their cropland.

Clash of the Extremes

Even though extremely little of the world's carbon emissions come from Bangladesh, the consequences the country faces from them are extremely harsh. You don't have to be a Supreme Court judge to know that's unfair. And Bangladesh is far from alone. Many other countries are caught in the same clash of extremes—Bolivia, the Maldives, the Marshall Islands, and Kiribati, just to name a few. Most are cash-poor, developing countries. Unlike the wealthy developed countries whose carbon emissions are extremely high, they can't afford to build costly projects and gizmos to adapt to and cope with the consequences. That's why the world needs to work together to cut down emissions and to respond to the climbing sea. To find out you what you can do, see page 50.

Rafting on a mattress might look like fun. But floods and rising seawater are no laughing matter in Bangladesh.

THE MARSHALL ISLANDS

GOING...GOING...GONE?

WHAT MAKES AN ISLAND AN ISLAND? It's surrounded by water, right? No wonder low-lying islands are at the greatest risk from the rising sea. It's easy to see how the sea could surge all over the Marshall Islands—which are made of sand and coral—and sweep them under its watery carpet.

⚓ HERE AND NOW

DUE TO CHANGING TRADE WINDS, the ocean is rising faster in the Marshall Islands than elsewhere on Earth. Over the last 30 years, water has jumped about a foot (0.3 m). That's about the distance from your ankles to your knees. Destructive signs of the rising sea are everywhere. Waves crash over crumbling seawalls built to keep water out. Seawater flows through the streets regularly and floods people's homes. And high tide creeps ever higher.

SPOTLIGHT ON ... THE MARSHALL ISLANDS

WHERE IN THE WORLD?
Pacific Ocean

HOME TO: 72,191 people

SIZE: 69.88 square miles
(181 sq km)

SEA-FEARING HEIGHTS:
most of its islands are
less than 6 feet (1.8 m)
above sea level

**BY 2100, SEA LEVEL
RISE MAY THREATEN:**
44,000 people

SLR GAME PLAN? A for
adapt, and **R** for relocate

PRICELESS TREASURE:
the world's largest
sanctuary for sharks

North Pacific Ocean

RONGELAP

WOTHO
LIKIEP
MEJIT
UJAE
KWAJALEIN
WOTJE
LAE
MALOELAP
LIB
NAMU
AUR
JABAT
AILINGLAPLAP
MAJURO
ARNO
JALUIT
MILI
NAMORIK
KILI
EBON

About 1,000 low-lying islands of
coral limestone and sand make
up the Marshall Islands. Most are
less than a mile (1.6 km) wide!

When the Sea Gets Rough, the Going Gets Tough...

. . ., and the tough get going. The Marshallese are fighting
back on all fronts. They're rebuilding seawalls to keep the
surging water out of their streets and homes. They're raising
funds for adaptation projects, such as building houses and
towns several feet above ground, and treatment plants to
clean fresh water contaminated by the rising sea. And many
Marshallese are moving to the United States. Unlike other
places under threat from the rising water, the Marshall
Islands has long-standing military ties to the States, which
allow the Marshallese to move there for a drier future.

▶▶ FAST FORWARD TO THE FUTURE

PEOPLE IN THE MARSHALL Islands
don't need a crystal ball to see their
watery future. Some say they feel
like they're living underwater already.
Even if the average global temperature
climbs only 3.6°F (2°C) and the sea
rises 1 to 4 feet (0.3–1.2 m), it might be
too late to save the Marshall Islands.
Some scientists think the rising water
will drown them, wiping the entire
country off the map.

KIRIBATI

ONCE THERE WERE 35 ISLANDS...

EVER BEEN IN A SITUATION where you felt extremely vulnerable—powerless to act without help, or open to attack? That's how Kiribati's leaders feel about sea level rise. They say their island nation is "among the most vulnerable of the vulnerable."

⚓ HERE AND NOW

TODAY, THERE ARE ONLY 33 ISLANDS. In 1999, the rising sea drowned two. Luckily, no one lived on those. But that's not the case for 21 of the remaining islands, especially South Tawara (see above), the capital island crammed with nearly half the nation's people. Much of Kiribati is less than 6.5 feet (2 m) above the sea. That's why it's so vulnerable. In some places, such as the village of Eita, people live right at sea level. And they're no strangers to flooding. In 2011, high tide swamped the houses in Eita and left villagers swimming in the streets.

⏩ FAST FORWARD TO THE FUTURE

IF GLOBAL SEA LEVELS RISE 3 to 6.5 feet (1–2 m) as predicted, much of Kiribati will be underwater. By the time you're grown up and have children who are about your age now, scientists think South Tawara will be unlivable. Today, islanders pile sandbags into seawalls and plant mangroves to cut down erosion. But the sea still rolls in, washing away the sandbag walls and flooding homes, soil, and water wells with salt water. No wonder the island nation has leased land in nearby Fiji, so its people have somewhere else to go.

Will Island Life Rock On?

Not all scientists think the rising sea will put Kiribati completely down for the count. Most of the nation's islands sit on top of coral reefs. Coral is a living thing that grows, moves, changes shape, and even responds to changes in the environment. During storms, waves wash sand inland over Kiribati. These blankets of sand are made of bits of coral shells, and they constantly build up the coral islands above the reef. Some scientists think this may help Kiribati stay above the rising water. But coral is extremely sensitive, and rising temperatures like those behind sea level rise can kill it off. So Kiribati might still end up in the drink. Stay tuned!

KIRIBATI

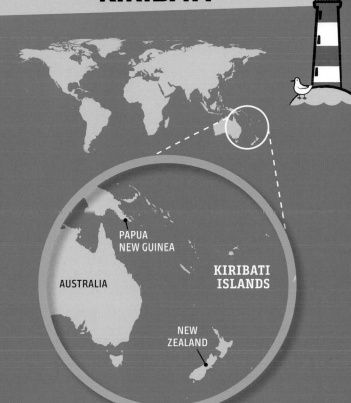

PAPUA NEW GUINEA

AUSTRALIA

KIRIBATI ISLANDS

NEW ZEALAND

Kiribati lies halfway between Hawaii and Australia. The nation of tiny islands has one of the largest ocean areas in the world.

WHERE IN THE WORLD?
Pacific Ocean

HOW IN THE WORLD DO YOU SAY ITS NAME?
KEE-ree-bahs

HOME TO: 105,711 people

SIZE: 313.13 square miles (811 sq km)

SEA-FEARING HEIGHTS: the nation's lowest point is sea level

BY 2100, SEA LEVEL RISE MAY THREATEN:
71,000 people

SLR GAME PLAN?
Relocate—move to higher ground

PRICELESS TREASURE:
Marawa, karawa, tarawa—in Kiribati, the words for "sea," "sky," and "land" rhyme, and the word *aba* means "land" as well as "people," showing that you can't have one without the other

ANTARCTICA

THE WILD CARD

HUGE! SUPERMASSIVE! GIANT! Antarctica has the largest single mass of ice on Earth. And it's like a wild card in a card game—you don't know if or when it might turn up, only that when it does, it's a game changer. For if this ice sheet goes into meltdown mode, global sea level could spike and then some. Check out the wild card of sea level rise.

SPOTLIGHT ON ...
ANTARCTICA

WHERE IN THE WORLD?
The South pole, at the "end of the world"

TEMPORARY HOME TO: research staff from 29 countries

SIZE: 5.4 million square miles (14 million sq km)

SEA-FEARING HEIGHTS:
0 feet (0 m) in some places

BY 2100, SEA LEVEL RISE MAY THREATEN: no permanent residents

SLR GAME PLAN? R for relocate and **A** for adapt

PRICELESS TREASURE: the Bentley Subglacial Trench—the deepest known ice and the lowest point on Earth that's not under the sea

Southern Ocean

ANTARCTICA

SOUTH POLE

PINE
ISLAND
ICE SHELF

Southern Ocean

The world's largest sheet of ice covers 98 percent of Antarctica.

⚓ HERE AND NOW

ANTARCTICA IS LIKE A GIANT FREEZER. Not only is the continent thickly coated in ice, but it's also the coldest, windiest, and driest place on Earth. No wonder no one lives there apart from researchers who study the place for short stints. Antarctica's ice sheet holds loads of frozen water—enough to raise global sea levels between 180 and 197 feet (55–60 m) if the whole thing melted. That's about the same height as 30 average NBA players stacked head to toe. The good news—if you can call it that—is that the ice sheet is unlikely to melt all at once. However, as early as 1995, scientists had begun to think that the globe's rising temperatures might be melting "chips off the old block"—parts of the ice sheet called "ice shelves" because they extend past the coast and float in water.

▶▶ FAST FORWARD TO THE FUTURE

IN 2015, an ice chunk as big as Chicago broke off the Pine Island Ice Shelf. Since it was already floating in the water, the huge chunk didn't raise the sea as it melted. But scientists noticed something strange. Instead of going to pieces at the edges, the ice shelf was busting up from within. In looking at satellite photos, they spied a crack that had opened up three years earlier at the base of the ice shelf some 20 miles (32 km) inland. This rift grew upward, and when it split open, the top of the ice shelf, the city-sized chunk, broke away. This crack and others like it were forming as warm seawater flowed into a seafloor canyon under the ice shelf, melting the belly of the ice. Scientists now predict that the Pine Island Ice Shelf will collapse, allowing ice from the West Antarctic ice sheet to slide off the land and into the ocean. That's because the ice shelf is like a cork in a bottle. Once it pops off, there's nothing to stop the ice behind it from flowing out. This, they say, could happen in our lifetime, raising sea levels almost 10 feet (3 m), flooding coastal cities around the world, such as New York, London, and Sydney.

Ice—the Wild Card

Predicting global sea level rise from climate change is tricky, especially based on the melting of ice sheets like the one in Antarctica. That's because ice can flow, crack, and break off in so many different ways, and scientists don't know much about how ice sheets melt. In particular, they don't know how much or how fast ice sheets might melt as global temperatures soar, and what, if any, conditions might trigger large chunks to collapse, slide into the sea, and melt. So no one knows how much of a part Antarctica or Greenland will play in sea level rise in the next 80 or so years. And since Antarctica's ice sheet holds so much frozen water, whatever part it plays can make or break the "game." How's that for a wild card?

WHAT YOU CAN DO

IN 2015, WORLD LEADERS AGREED to fight the soaring temperatures that propel sea level rise by keeping global warming "well below" 3.6°F (2°C). But even that might not be enough to save low-lying islands like the Marshall Islands and the Maldives, or the mangrove forest of Bangladesh. So they agreed to try to keep warming to 2.7°F (1.5°C). Sounds good, but unfortunately, they had no clear plan for doing this. It's up to us to hold them to this agreement and to do our part to reduce carbon emissions. Here are 10 things you can do.

1 SPEAK UP!

VOICE YOUR CONCERNS and the steps you want the world to take to cut down on the carbon emissions that fuel rising temperatures and sea level rise. Talk to friends, family, and neighbors as well as local and world leaders.

2 REDUCE, REUSE, RECYCLE

YOU KNOW THE DRILL, RIGHT? So just do it. That way, you can help cut down the energy we use to make new goods and, in turn, the carbon we emit.

3 STOP HOGGING ENERGY

FAR BE IT FROM YOU to leave the lights on when you leave a room—oh no, not you! But have you replaced light bulbs with compact fluorescent lights or LEDs? Do you wash clothes in cold or warm water rather than hot, and then hang them to dry rather than running the dryer?

4 BE A WATER SCROOGE

PUMPING, TREATING, and heating water sucks up lots of energy. The less water you use, the less energy we burn and, you got it, the less carbon emitted. Don't let faucets drip, turn off the faucet while you brush your teeth, and wash dishes and clothes only when you have full load.

5 BE A CLEAN, GREEN POWER CHAMP

CHOOSE SOLAR, WIND, or other renewable kinds of power when you and your family have a choice. And if your local power company doesn't give you a choice, ask them to—and keep asking until they do.

6 POWER DOWN AND UNPLUG

POWERING DOWN is only the first step. Even though that video game dashboard, cellphone charger, and MP3 player might not look like they're up to much when they're turned off, they're still sucking energy. Unplug them to cut off power and, in turn, power down sea level rise.

7 WALK, CYCLE, SKATEBOARD, OR BLADE

NOT ONLY CAN YOU get around on your own steam, but you can also help fight sea level rise along the way. The second-biggest source of carbon emissions in the United States and Canada comes from cars, trucks, buses, planes, and trains. So the next time you want a drive, take your legs for a spin instead.

BURP!

9 EAT LESS MEAT

RAISING LIVESTOCK for meat and dairy products requires more energy than producing other food. What's more, as cows fart and belch, they release methane gas, which adds to global warming. How's that for raising a big stink?

8 EAT LOCAL, SHOP LOCAL

WHEN YOU EAT LOCALLY grown foods, you cut down the distance that food travels from the farm to your mouth. That way, less carbon is emitted by cars, trucks, planes, and trains to transport the food. Buying locally made clothes, bikes, furniture, and other goods cuts down carbon emissions the same way.

10 BE A BACKYARD SCIENTIST

Keep your eye on the sea and bounce back what you see. Nowadays, scientists ask ordinary people to look around their backyard, neighborhood, or community and tell them what changes they see from rising water levels and rising temperatures. Go online to find out how you can take part. And remember, one of the best ways to keep your ahead above water is to stay informed.

GLOSSARY

adaptation
an adjustment of action, or process, to work with changes in the environment

Anthropocene
coined from the Greek words for "human being" and "new" to describe a new time in Earth's history in which human activities are a major force affecting the environment and climate of the planet

artifact
a human-made object, such as a tool, weapon, or jewelry, usually from another time and/or culture in history

atmosphere
a thin layer of gases around Earth that traps heat from the Sun, without which life as we know it could not exist on our planet

bay
a wide area of the sea where the land curves inward

bedrock
solid rock that lies under soil

carbon
a substance that occurs naturally in the universe and is a basic building block of stars, planets, and all living things

carbon dioxide (CO$_2$)
a colorless, odorless gas made of molecules that contain one carbon atom and two oxygen atoms

carbon emissions
carbon dioxide and carbon monoxide given off into the atmosphere as coal, oil, and natural gas are burned for energy

climate
an area's expected weather over a long time, such as a cold, snowy winter or a hot, dry summer

climate change
a change in the usual weather of a place, such as a rise in temperature or rainfall

delta
land at the mouth of a river formed out of sand, silt, clay, and gravel left by the flowing water; often formed where the river splits into streams and often shaped like a triangle

dike
a long wall, or bank of earth or stone, made to stop flooding from the sea or a river

THE CARBON CYCLE
Check out how carbon "fuels" life on Earth:

1. Carbon is in the air. It's part of carbon dioxide (CO_2)—one of the gases in the atmosphere around Earth.

2. Plants and trees "breathe in" CO_2 and "breathe out" oxygen (O_2). They mix CO_2 with water and sunlight to make sugar called carbohydrates. These carbohydrates contain energy that plants and trees use to grow and live.

3. Animals, including humans, breathe in O_2 and breathe out CO_2. They also eat plants and/or other animals. And the carbohydrates in those plants and animals give them energy to grow and live.

4. When plants and animals die, their bodies break down in the ground. Over millions of years, heat and pressure from the Earth form their remains into hydrocarbons, such as oil, gas, and coal—a.k.a. fossil fuels.

5. And what do we use fossil fuels for? You got it—energy! We burn fossil fuels to light the world, run cars, and heat our homes. Burning fossil fuels releases CO_2, which builds up, making the atmosphere thicker. The atmosphere then traps more heat from the Sun and the Earth becomes hotter. Over time, this can change the climate around the world.

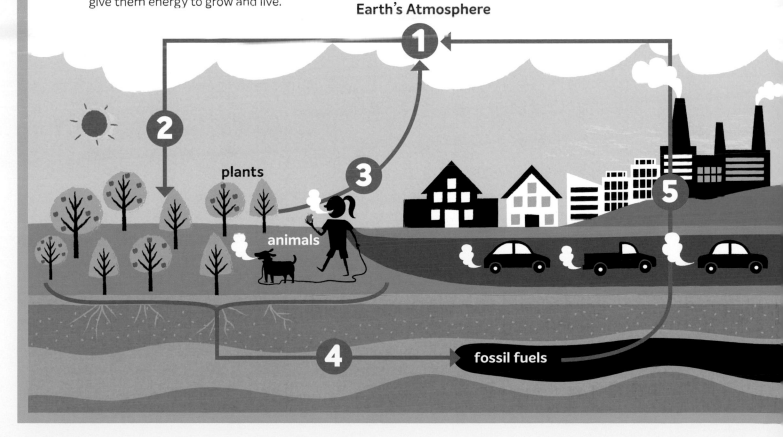

Earth's Atmosphere

plants

animals

fossil fuels

GLOSSARY

drone
a remote-controlled flying machine, such as a camera; some drones fly and operate on their own

ecosystem
all the living things, such as plants and animals, that share an environment

First Nation
a community of people who have lived in an area since ancient times known as "time immemorial"

fossil fuel
a fuel, such as coal, oil, or natural gas, formed long, long ago from the remains of living things

glacier
a thick, slow-moving body or river of ice formed by the build up of snow

global warming
a long-lasting rise in Earth's average temperature

greener
more friendly for the environment

Gulf Stream
a warm ocean current from the Gulf of Mexico that flows past the east coast of North America and crosses the Atlantic Ocean to northwestern Europe

high tide
the highest level of the tide, the regular rising and falling of the sea

high-water mark
the highest level of the sea at high tide

Ice Age
a time in Earth's history when ice sheets covered large areas of the planet's surface

ice cap
a cover of ice over a big area less than 12 million acres (50,000 sq km), such as the poles at the north and south ends of the Earth

ice sheet
a thick layer of ice that covers a large area greater than 12 million acres (50,000 sq km) for a long time

ice shelf
a floating ice sheet attached to land

Indigenous peoples
peoples who are native to a place, who have lived there since ancient times known as "time immemorial"

ocean current
a large body of water like a river that flows from place to place through the ocean

renewable

an energy source that continually renews, or resupplies, itself, such as wind, water, or solar energy

sand dune

a mound or small hill of sand formed by wind near the coast or in a desert

sea level

the height of the surface of the sea

sea level rise (SLR)

when the surface of the sea moves higher

seawall

a wall or bank of earth built to stop the sea from flowing in and moving in on land

simulation

a model or imitation of how a real-world process or system behaves

Sphinx

an ancient Egyptian statue of a lion's body with a human head

trade winds

steady winds blowing at sea from east to west near the Equator

vapor

a gaseous form of a substance, such as water, spread throughout air

water (H_2O)

a colorless, odorless liquid made of molecules that contain two hydrogen atoms and one oxygen atom

Flip to page 50 to learn about the water cycle!

weather

the temperature, rain, wind, and other atmospheric conditions that pop up in an area from minute to minute or day to day

World Bank

an international bank that loans money to countries around the world to help them develop and rebuild

THE WATER CYCLE
Check out how water's always on the go:

2

FORMING CLOUDS

In the atmosphere, the water vapor cools, turning into water drops. Large groups of water drops form clouds.

3

1

GOING UP

The Sun warms the top of the ocean. The warm ocean water evaporates—turning from liquid to vapor. The water vapor rises up into the atmosphere.

FALLING DOWN

Rain or snow falls from the clouds. Some falls into the ocean, some onto land. On land, some of this water runs off into rivers and streams that flow into the ocean. And some seeps into the ground, flowing into underground lakes or the ocean.

4

GOING BACK 'ROUND

And the water cycle begins again.

Books

Green, Dan. Climate Change: A Hot Topic. London, U.K.: Toucan Books, 2014.

Klein, Grady, and Yoram Bauman. The Cartoon Introduction to Climate Change. Washington, D.C.: Island Press, 2014.

Sneideman, Joshua, and Erin Twamley. Climate Change: Discover How It Impacts Spaceship Earth. White River Junction, VT: Nomad Press, 2015.

Websites

Climate Kids: NASA's Eyes on the Earth

https://climatekids.nasa.gov/health-report-sea-level/

National Geographic: Sea Level Rise

http://www.nationalgeographic.com/environment/global-warming/sea-level-rise/

National Ocean Service

https://oceanservice.noaa.gov/facts/sealevelclimate.html

NOAA Sea Level Rise Viewer

https://coast.noaa.gov/digitalcoast/tools/slr

Surging Seas

http://sealevel.climatecentral.org/

Movie

An Inconvenient Sequel: Truth to Power

https://inconvenientsequel.tumblr.com/

INDEX

Page numbers in **bold** denote definitions.
Page numbers in *italics* denote maps or
  photographs.

INDEX

PHOTO CREDITS